Urbanisation in India

BASIC SERVICES AND PEOPLE'S PARTICIPATION

INSTITUTE OF SOCIAL SCIENCES
URBAN STUDIES SERIES

I. Urbanisation in Developing Countries: Basic Services and Community Participation
Edited by **Bidyut Mohanty**

II. Urbanisation in India: Basic Services and People's Participation
by **K. C. Sivaramakrishnan, Biplab Dasgupta, M. N. Buch**

III. Basic Services for Urban Poor: Case of Baroda, Bhilwara, Sambalpur, Siliguri
by **Archana Ghosh, S. Sami Ahmad, Shipra Maitra**

IV. Rapid Urbanisation and Access to Basic Services in India: A Status Report

Urban Studies Series No. 2

Urbanisation in India

BASIC SERVICES AND PEOPLE'S PARTICIPATION

K. C. SIVARAMAKRISHNAN
BIPLAB DASGUPTA
M. N. BUCH

with an Introduction by
Heinz Bongartz

INSTITUTE OF SOCIAL SCIENCES, NEW DELHI
and
CONCEPT PUBLISHING COMPANY, NEW DELHI

ISBN 81-7022-480-2

First Published 1993
Reprint 1996

Published by
Ashok Kumar Mittal
Concept Publishing Company
A/15-16 Commercial Block
Mohan Garden
New Delhi 110 059

Layout by
Institute of Social Sciences
B-7/18 Safdarjung Enclave
New Delhi 110 029

Contents

Foreword

This publication, the second in the series on urban studies, includes contributions by three well-known specialists in urban affairs. These writings were originally key-note addresses delivered at three seminars organized by the Institute of Social Sciences in co-operation with Friedrich Ebert Stiftung: Mr K. C. Sivaramakrishnan's at the international seminar on "Basic Amenities in the Context of Rapid Urbanisation: Drinking Water and Sanitation Issues" in New Delhi (November 1991), Prof. Biplab Dasgupta's at the Eastern Region Seminar on "Urban Basic Services and Local Participation" in Bhubaneswar (November 1992) and Mr M. N. Buch's at the Western Region Seminar on the same theme in Baroda (April 1993). These three presentations are important contributions in the current debate on and search for solutions to some of the pressing urban problems facing India and other developing countries.

I am grateful to Dr. Heinz Bongartz, Resident Representative of the Friedrich Ebert Stiftung, New Delhi, and a scholar in his own right, for writing the introduction to this book and to the Friedrich Ebert Stiftung for their sustained support to the urban studies projects of the Institute.

New Delhi
June 1, 1993

George Mathew
Director

Introduction

Disadvantaged sections of the population in developing countries live in rural as well as in urban areas. In the past, it was always believed that the urban areas would develop automatically, whereas concerted efforts would have to be made to plan the development of the rural areas. However, socio-political and developmental arguments are now frequently put forward for the uplift of disadvantaged sections of the urban population as well. These arguments are based on facts which simply cannot be ignored. First, we have acute poverty in urban areas, since the urban poor cannot fall back on their own land for the production of food to meet their minimum subsistence requirements. Second, the urban people are completely dependent on those who own the means of production. And finally, there is a higher degree of consciousness among the urban population facilitating its organisation and mobilisation in the struggle for social change.

In India, economic development during the past four decades since the inception of planning has resulted in a little increase in average per capita income. There is no doubt that living conditions have improved everywhere, even in the most backward districts. Yet, a large number of people have remained poor, deprived of basic nutrition, rudimentary shelter, minimally competent medical attention and primary education. The existence of poverty is incompatible with the vision of an advanced, prosperous, democratic, egalitarian and just society implied in the concept of a socialist pattern of society. Elimination of poverty, therefore, must be the highest priority of society.

Urban poverty is one area which needs special attention. As per the Planning Commission's definition of the poverty line, about 19 per cent of the population in urban areas is living below the poverty line. This does not mean that the remaining 80 per cent or so has access to adequate urban basic services like housing, water supply, sanitation, education, health care, etc. The rapid rise in the urban population has been a definite cause for the deterioration in urban living conditions. India's urban population which was 79 million in 1961 has now risen to 220 million in 1992. The urban population by the turn of the century is likely to be 315 to 325 million. The number of million plus cities is also likely to more than double from 23 at present to 49 by the year 2001. This tremendous increase in urban population is certainly going to aggravate the problem of already precarious living conditions of a large chunk of the population. The absolute magnitude of the growth of the urban population is so large that a close new look at the existing policies concerned with urban development is needed. No doubt, agricultural and rural development will continue to be priority areas as regards planning. However, in spite of best efforts to improve the condition of rural masses, large scale migration from rural to urban areas will continue to take place in the coming decades.

In a developing country like India, urbanisation takes place as a natural consequence of economic changes. At the same time, urbanisation helps to contribute to the growth process at large. This is indicated by the increasing contribution of the urban sector to national income. The contribution of the urban sector to the gross domestic product [GDP] which was a mere 29 per cent in 1950-51 increased to 47 per cent in 1980-81 and is estimated to rise to about 60 per cent by the turn of the century. However, this positive role of urbanisation in India is overshadowed by the increase in urban poverty. There is evident deterioration in the physical environment and quality of life in the urban areas caused by the widening gap between demand and supply of essential services and infrastructure. Increasing pressure of population, particularly its concentration in large cities and metros, and escalating per capita cost of providing urban services account for deterioration of infrastructure services and amenities. The worst sufferers are the poor, whose access to the basic services like drinking water, sanitation, education and basic health services, is shrinking. The government's investment in urban infrastructure has also been less than adequate. In the central budget allocation for 1993-94, only about one per cent of total central plan outlay has been earmarked for urban development. Keeping in view the challenge of reorientating the urbanisation process by overcoming infrastructural deficiencies, this amount will not be enough to take the best advantage of economic growth inherent in urbanisation. The gap between demand and supply of infrastructural services will continue to widen.

Urban settlements, by their very nature, need a minimum of basic services for their healthy existence. However, the state of most of India's urban areas in this respect is far from satisfactory. Many of the municipal bodies are being badly administered, have underdeveloped or eroded tax systems and lack adequate capital funds for development. The services, where provided have deteriorated over the years and there seems no sign of reversal. Overcrowded and under-serviced, increasing portions of most urban areas are turning into slums. In view of the extremely serious situation in which urban bodies find themselves, a vigorous multi-pronged attack is needed to reverse the trend and restore conditions of healthy growth.

In fulfilling the basic needs of the population, housing ranks next only to food and clothing in importance. A certain minimum standard of housing, therefore, must enjoy high priority in a society like India's where housing amenities are far below the minimum standards that have been internationally accepted. Housing activity serves to fulfil many of the fundamental objectives of planning in India: providing shelter; raising the quality of life, particularly of the poorer sections of the population; creating conditions which are conducive to the achievement of crucial objectives in terms of health, sanitation and education; creating substantial additional employment and dispersed economic activity; improving urban-rural and inter-personal equity through the narrowing down of differences in standards of living and last, but not the least, generating additional voluntary savings.

In fact, housing does not mean merely providing a roof. It means much more. While talking about the Right to Shelter, an eminent jurist of India, Justice P. P. Sawant mentioned:

> Shelter for a human being is not mere protection for his life and limb. It is in his home where he has opportunities to grow physically, mentally, intellectually and spiritually. Right to shelter, therefore, includes right to adequate living space, safe and decent structure, clean and decent surroundings, sufficient light, pure air and water, electricity, sanitation and drainage facilities, roads and transport, educational and recreational facilities and easy and quick access to the workplace and to the provisions of life. The right to shelter thus does not mean a mere right to a roof over one's head, but a right to the entire infrastructure necessary to enable man to live and develop as a human being.

The total backlog of housing in urban India was estimated to be 10.4 million in 1991. It is also estimated that about 48.8 million persons were living in slums in 1990. The situation is serious and needs the urgent attention of planners and decision-makers.

Inadequate provision of water and sanitation is another serious problem of the urban poor. The daily per capita availability of water in class I cities (population of 100,000 and above) of India averages 142 liters. A considerable number of cities have only 50 litres of water available per capita per day. As against this supply, the average demand is 231 litres per day – a shortfall of 89 litres per capita per day in class I cities. The urban poor, due to their low paying capacity and also due to the peculiar conditions governing their settlement patterns, are generally deprived of adequate water and sanitation facilities. The high incidence of death and disease in urban poor settlements can be attributed largely to the poor quality of water and sanitation facilities. This is another serious problem of the urban poor.

Urban transport is another area of concern in India. The transport problems of urban areas, and specially those of the metropolises, have so far not received due attention. Meanwhile, traffic has continued to multiply with the result that the urban transport infrastructure in almost all large cities is on the verge of breakdown. In the absence of reliable public transport, people are compelled to resort to private vehicles, which has aggravated congestion, pollution and energy consumption. There is no single agency to plan, coordinate or execute transport policies and programmes in urban areas.

Today, urban managers are facing a gigantic task. They need to give top priority to a variety of policy decisions and implement a wide range of programmes. With the growth and expansion of cities, people's aspirations and expectations also rise which can ultimately become a major problem for urban managers, if not taken cognizance of. They need to orient themselves to face a challenging task ahead, perhaps with the help of some useful guiding material and training.

Heinz Bongartz
Resident Representative
Friedrich Ebert Stiftung
New Delhi

1

Water and Sanitation Facilities in Urban India: Issues Concerning Management and Finance

K. C. Sivaramakrishnan

The Overview

The pace and volume of urbanisation across the world and in developing countries has been documented extensively and no purpose will be served by repeating them here. Cities are no longer a western phenomenon. They are very much a part of the demographic and economic change which is swiftly and irreversibly altering the landscape of developing countries. Asia contained some of the most ancient cities of the world – Beijing, Patliputra, Babylon, Samarkand and Isfahan are some of the many names which conjure up memories of great civilisations and mercantile glory. But until this century the spread of urbanisation has not been a significant phenomenon. Today, half of the East Asia's population is urban. South Asia's urban population has also increased from 17 per cent in 1960 to about 24 per cent in 1980. As of now, out of 2.2 billion people in Asia, a quarter live in urban areas. By the end of the century it is estimated that the Asian population will surpass three billion and that the urban population will itself be close to a billion. In absolute numbers, countries like China and India will have urban populations far above the total population of several countries.

Key-note address delivered at the International Seminar on "Access to Basic Amenities in the Context of Rapid Urbanisation: Drinking Water and Sanitation Issues" organised by the Institute of Social Sciences in New Delhi, November 1991.

Yet the paradox is that China and India, as well as some other Asian countries will still be regarded as largely rural or agricultural. This is not a game of names or numbers. After all, when the size of the urban population is 217 million as in India and the number of cities and towns well over 5,000, there is little point in citing the rural population of 627 million and taking comfort in the statement that 'India lives in its villages'. Of course it does. But is it not time for us to accept that India lives also in its cities and towns?

Suggestions continue to be made of slower urbanisation, pointing out that the decennial growth of urban population in India during the period 1981-91 has been 36.19 per cent compared to 46.14 per cent in the 1971-81 decade. This is a rather misleading and somewhat mistaken conclusion. Since 1921 the rate of urban growth has been well above the overall growth percentage and in some decades nearly two or three times more. Even during the 1981-91 decade the urban growth percentage of 36.19 has been much higher than the overall growth rate of 23.56. Since independence urban population in the country has almost quadrupled. In 1951 it was 62 million. The urban growth rates are much higher in the agriculturally advanced States such as Punjab and Haryana as well as in the States such as Karnataka and Maharashtra than rest of the country. The Indian experience only confirms the well known trend that agricultural development, better farm productivity, rising farm incomes as also the limitations in absorbing the growing labour force in agriculture, all contribute to an increase in urbanisation. I have elaborated on the Indian phenomenon because I feel the problem of urbanisation and the provision of services for the urban population are as much of perception, as of lack of resources.

Status of Water Supply and Sanitation

The global consultation on Safe Water and Sanitation which met here in Delhi in September 1990 started its proceedings on the modest note that globally the percentage of population covered by water supply increased from 44 to 69 per cent, which was largely due to progress made in the rural areas. On the other hand, the urban unserved increased by some 31 million, reflecting the position in Africa, Asia and the Pacific.

A part of the problem in measuring coverage is that the data are limited to simple arithmetics. Usually most national reports describe the total population of a whole town as 'covered' if there is some kind of water supply system functioning in the city. Per capita figures of supply are calculated even more simplistically by dividing the total installed capacity by population. We need not go very far to search for the truth. In Delhi itself the per capita water supply as officially reported is about 200 litres per day. This comfortable average, however, doesn't mean much to about 30 per cent of the city's nine million people who have access if at all to about 25 litres or less. Even in cities claiming 100 per cent reach, the per capita availability varies as much as 10 times between marginal settlements and the so-called better-off localities. The inequities in distribution are not just a statistical problem. They seriously distort tariffs and jeopardise cost recovery, apart from creating a sense of complacency in the minds of the decision-makers.

The coverage in regard to sanitation is even worse. The UNDP estimates that during the International Water Supply and Sanitation Decade, an estimated 748 million people received access to sanitation: 314 million in the urban areas and 434 million in the rural, due mainly to the large gains made in rural sanitation in Asia and the Pacific. Though in percentage terms coverage in urban areas rose from 69 to 72 per cent, in absolute terms, those left unserved rose from 292 to 377 million.

Perception of the Need

Most public policy or plan documents of most developing countries regard water supply and sanitation as "basic amenities". Yet this exalted position is not reflected in their budget allocations. What the Human Development Report of the UNDP terms as 'the human expenditure ratio' which is a percentage of national income devoted to human priority concerns, continues to be low in many developing countries and in some is probably going to be less. In the grim economic scenario which faces many countries burdened by external debt, adverse trade conditions, low economic growth and compulsions of security and defence, public expenditure on these human priority concerns such as primary education, health care and water and sanitation are first and easy casualties of budget exercises.

The comparison between rural and urban needs further exacerbates the problem. In India as well as some other developing countries, there is a needless but continuing preoccupation with comparisons of the severity of deprivation among the rural and urban poor. The Human Development Report has also presented an index of rural-urban disparity. Taking the urban average of access as 100, the HDR reports the disparity as 62 for water and 45 for sanitation. I respectfully submit these comparisons do not serve much purpose. I have already mentioned the all too simplistic and highly inadequate reporting on coverage of water supply. The figures are also not sensitive to the high density of urban settlements, in particular, the towns where congestion aggravates poor services. The mosquito that carries malaria or filaria or the water-borne germs spreading cholera, do not respect municipal boundaries nor urban-rural divisions. Morbidity characteristics tend to be rather similar and in fact in urban concentrations, the prevalence of gastro-enteric diseases and jaundice is more pronounced. There is little point in comparing gross supply figures. The urban poor are as badly off as the rural poor in terms of quantity and quality of services as well as the time and effort spent in access to them.

A part of the problem in many countries is that water supply and sanitation are regarded as social sectors not directly connected to the production sectors of the country. The economic impact of poor water supply and sanitation is rarely understood and usually not quantified. In recent years as part of an increasing awareness of gender issues, studies have been undertaken in several countries to assess the time and effort that women and children have to spend to secure fuel and water for the household. In a recent study of Delhi, Hyderabad and Ghaziabad in India, Vinay Lal reports that on an average a woman has to spend 3.8 hours per day in fetching water for the household. Anyone who has seen the long queues of buckets and jerry cans in the slums of Manila, Bangkok or elsewhere should have no problem in understanding what this time and effort means in terms of lost wages.

The Future Demand

The projections for 2000 and beyond indicate that of the world urban population of 3.7 billion, 2.2 billion may be in developing countries. In the African region the anticipated urban growth rate of 5.4 per cent will take the urban population to over 250 million, almost twice the number as was in 1988. Urban Asia will be about 880 million. As for urban poverty estimates, it is expected that the percentage of urban poor will decline slightly from 28 to 24 per cent. However, their absolute numbers are estimated to rise by nearly one-third from the current estimate of 330 million to 430 million. This assumes of course that per capita income growth will be similar to the levels as between 1965 and 1986. A more pessimistic assumption could give substantially higher numbers.

It is important to emphasize that it is not urbanisation which has caused or increased poverty. Cities have not invented poverty, they have only made it more visible. But this visibility should not prompt leaders and decision-makers to close their eyes or flee the scene. Given the severe crunch on resources and the anticipated increase in numbers, we have to focus on critical issues of technology, finance and management.

The Issues

First, we have to recognize that at the present rates of consumption, over-use and wastage, many countries are literally running out of water. As it is, in Mexico, India, Pakistan and China, water-tables are dropping. In 1975, as many as 19 countries were classified as having less than 500 cubic metres of renewable water per person per year. After accounting for losses, this means an availability of 200 cubic metres per capita, which is not sufficient to meet domestic and irrigation water-supply demands. By 2000, ten more countries will be added to this problem list. If the present trend continues, nearly 40 countries will have a serious problem. The question is not how much water is needed but rather how best the water demand can be managed and how to optimise the use of available water.

Though only seven per cent of the world's water is used for domestic demands and 70 per cent for irrigation, the efficiency of water used in agriculture in most countries is around 30 per cent only. The inefficiency is no less in urban areas. Leakage and unaccounted for water in many cities in many countries is 40 per cent. Distribution arrangements and existing tariff systems have hardly any relevance for water conservation, wastage reduction or recycling. This is as much an issue of technology application as of management.

In large cities, the cost of conveyance and distribution has become very high. The dependability of large-scale systems is also getting to be less. At the risk of offending public health engineers and those favouring large-scale water supply authorities, I would suggest a closer scrutiny of the limits of such large-scale systems. In cities like Manila, Calcutta, Shanghai or Cairo, are we sure that the economies of scale continue to be valid? Should we not explore the possibility of disaggregated supply arrangements which can be more sensitive to local needs and more easily managed at the local level?

Yet another issue of technology is the type of supply and sources within the urban settlement, particularly the periurban settlements and slums. The hand-pump has been heralded all over the world as having vastly improved access to water. Yet in urban areas, given the concentration of population and the very poor sanitation, hand-pump sources have also been easily exposed to contamination. The gastroenteritis epidemic in the slum settlements in Delhi in 1988 clearly established this.

Global warming, diminishing rain forests, protection of the ozone layer and preserving genetic diversity are all hot subjects of discussion today but closer to the ground is the problem of water pollution. The contamination of water resources is now wide spread in many developing countries, brought about by industrialisation as well as untreated sewage. In India 70 per cent of the total surface waters are considered to be polluted. The UNDP reports that in China out of 78 rivers monitored, 54 are reported to be seriously polluted by untreated sewage and industrial waste. Several rivers in Malaysia are devoid of fish and aquatic animals.

Surface water pollution is also a major problem affecting rural water supply sources. I am personally hopeful that strict adherence to the principle "pollutor pays" as well as the adoption of clean technologies will help us overcome the problem of water pollution from industrial sources. I am, however, much less hopeful about treatment of domestic sewage. Most of the Class I cities in India do not have a sewerage system at all. Even in the so-called metropolitan cities of more than a million population, only 50 per cent of the waste water is collected and treated partially or otherwise. Unfortunately, the costs of conventional sewerage system continue to be very high and the level of technology developed and application effort limited. While man has succeeded in putting one of his species on the Moon, he has not been able to deal with his own waste in an efficient, cost effective manner. Technologies like anaerobic treatment and those for recovery of resources from sewage continue to be applied on a limited scale only.

The Ganga Action Plan launched in this country in 1985 was the first comprehensive plan of action to address, in an integrated manner, conveyance and treatment of sewage, resource recovery through methane gas, fish-farming and irrigation, sustaining aquatic diversity, and river quality monitoring and management. But the plan is limited only to the Ganga.

Low-cost sanitation with pit latrines or pour-flush latrines has definitely helped to improve the sanitation coverage but there are serious limitations in adopting this approach everywhere. In India a major programme has been launched to provide low-cost sanitation wherever feasible in towns having a population of up to 500,000. The programme is an imaginative combination of loans, grants and beneficiary contributions, involving local bodies and aiming at the elimination of manual scavenging. Work is in progress in over 400 towns at a cost of Rs. 155 million. Under this programme, about 78,000 pour-flush toilets are being built. A complementary programme will help rehabilitate about 30,000 scavengers through retraining and placement in other occupations. Successive governments have continued to give top priority to this particular programme which demonstrates what can be accomplished if different departments and levels of the government can get their act together.

Financing

It is estimated that during the International Water Supply and Sanitation Decade, various governments and external support agencies spent about $ 120 billion which amounts to approximately $ 100 for each additional person served during the decade. These are according to 1985 prices. If the investment levels are not increased considerably in the 1990s to provide water supply and sanitation, the per capita expenditure may come down.

What then are the possible courses of action? Consider the following:

Should we strive to lower the cost further?
How much can we recover from the user?
Can we draw on private resources not used before? and
How can public expenditure allocations be increased?

I have already touched upon the need for cost reduction and cost effectiveness. Technology application, extension of trained man power to build and maintain water supply and sanitation installations are all crucial. The plumber, whether in the United States or elsewhere, is an expensive and difficult person to get hold of. Our experience in low cost sanitation indicates how important it is to develop easily understood methods of latrine construction. Some of the public authorities, as in Tamil Nadu, have brought out handy little folders with pictures to describe the process. Still, for the average city dweller, the construction of a latrine is a complex and difficult business.

The position is much worse regarding water supply. Quality control in the sinking of hand-pumps and their efficient operation and maintenance on a large enough scale are important aspects. As for piped systems the net cost of production is increasing and currently averaging about 25 to 30 cents per kilo litre. While the Decade has provided a broad range of low cost technologies, scaling up is an important task which is pending.

The poor cost recovery should not give one the impression that there is no potential to pay at all. Even in slum settlements it is seen that about 40 per cent of the families do make some form of payment which is often more than what the higher income groups pay. The remaining households will also be prepared to pay for improved supply. Cost recovery mechanisms tend to rely heavily on individual metering and billing. The Kumpung Improvement Programme, Basti Improvement Schemes or Urban Basic Services are examples of converging basic amenities and services. This area-based approach for provision of services has to be taken further towards operations and maintenance and cost recovery.

However, faced by the stark reality of declining budget allocations, local bodies and water authorities have of late begun to look for loan grant combinations. During the past one year, India's Housing and Urban Development Corporation, 'a parastatal', has sanctioned 54 projects for water supply and sewage in different cities at a total cost of about Rs. 800 crores. HUDCO itself is providing a loan of Rs. 330 crores on rates of interest varying 12 to 15.5 per cent. The bulk of the amount is for eight projects in some metropolitan cities. The significance of the HUDCO initiative is that it marks a departure from total dependence on public exchequer allocations.

Management

The role of urban local bodies in providing water supply and sanitation has varied from country to country. While in Latin America these are understood and accepted as patently municipal functions, there has been much ambivalence in Asia and Africa. Arguments about resource mobilization and the so-called efficiency considerations have led to the water supply function being taken away from municipal bodies in many countries. A study of 29 cities by the Operations Research Group in India indicates that as many as 22 provincial level bodies took up the capital works but only in five were they involved in operation and maintenance. The division between capital works and operational and management responsibilities has been a long-standing problem. If public accountability, better understanding of local needs and flexibility in delivery arrangements are required, there is, perhaps, no substitute for local bodies.

Unfortunately in many of our countries, decentralisation has been a tenuous and uncertain exercise. In spite of the vast and dramatic changes in the economy and political structure of many societies, the orthodox nation-state model, relying on external sovereignty against transnational influences and internal sovereignty against local and regional powers, continues to influence many minds. Recent events, however, show that even the largest country is too small to govern the world and at the same time too large to govern their cities. What holds for the USA and New York is as much true of Tokyo or Seoul, Shanghai and Jakarta, Bombay or Lagos.

There is, therefore, no escape or alternative to decentralisation. In a situation of rising aspirations, limited resources and the near impossible task of rational, happy national budgets and self-expanding bureaucracies, decentralisation may indeed be the only approach to sustain large societies within some acceptable frame of government. Akin Mabogunje the renowned African scholar refers to the perception of central and provincial governments as fountainheads of patronage: the obvious fear is that decentralisation would cause hydraulic problems to the fountain. We have to get over these apprehensions and accept that local participation, through local governments as well as community participation, is as much a financial necessity.

The decade of the 1980s has been an extremely difficult one for domestic resource mobilisation and expenditure. It has not also been a bright period for external resource mobilisation. In fact, from 1986 to 1988 the net outflow from heavily indebted countries was over 100 billion dollars. The recent World Debt Tables confirm this sad trend and it is feared that many countries pay about five per cent of GDP in debt repayments. No one knows for certain how much governments in developing countries are spending on water supply and sanitation. It is estimated that the current levels of investment in the sector are about $ 10 billion. The New Delhi Consultation last year concluded that a five-fold increase in that amount would be needed to provide water supply and sanitation to all by the year 2000. William Draper, the UNDP Administrator in his forthright opening address, suggested that a $ 50 billion a year might be called unrealistic but $ 15 to $ 20 billion a year would not. Perhaps he is right: perhaps not. But $ 50 billion is what it took to wage the 15-day war in the Gulf.

2

Delivery of Urban Basic Services: Issues in People's Participation

Biplab Dasgupta

At the very outset, let me thank you for giving me this opportunity to deliver the key-note address to this very important gathering of social scientists and experts on urban issues. The subject of the seminar covers a vast ground, and I do not feel competent to critically examine all the aspects of this highly important as well as sensitive issue. All that I propose to do here is to generalize on some of the major aspects of the delivery of urban services, to identify some of the major economic, social, administrative and other constraints, and then to put forward some views, very personal views, on the question of local level participation. I would be grateful if at least some of the questions I am raising are discussed and debated over the next three days.

The first point that strikes me is the utter inadequacy of these services – transport, water supply, sewerage and drainage, garbage disposal, power, to name some of the major ones – in relation to the need of the urban population. Of course, estimates of urban need are not easy. International norms tend to be too high and are not achievable within the foreseeable future. Within the

---

Key-note address delivered at the Eastern Region seminar on "Urban Basic Services and Local Participation" organised by the Institute of Social Sciences in Bhubaneswar, November 1992.

country, norms adopted for the metropolises cannot be applied to smaller towns and settlements. Such difficulties remain. A great deal of research would be necessary to establish a set of norms for various types of settlements for each of these services, which would be achievable, but, at the same time, would not be too conservative to allow for only a limited account of progress. But, no matter what norms are adopted and how, the fact remains, based on popular perception as well as comparative evaluation of those who have widely travelled, that our cities and towns appear to be overcrowded, our transport network suffers from interminable traffic jams, our water supply does not meet the minimum needs of bathing, cleaning, washing and cooking, most of our sewers, where they exist, are exposed and smelly, water-logging is endemic during the rainy season, solid waste overflows the dustbins, and loadshedding is a regular feature of daily existence during most of the year in most of the cities.

Second, whatever services exist, their actual deliveries to the citizenry, in terms of both quality and quantity, are far less than the capacities that have been created, both in terms of machine and manpower. Leakages are widespread, and these are not confined to water mains. In Calcutta, about one-third of the capacity for water supply is wasted along the transmission line, but no less serious is the choking of the underground sewer to the extent of one-third of its capacity because of silt formation. The full width of a road is never put to use, as a part is taken up by pedestrian overflow, another by street vendors and parked cars, while bad road maintenance makes another part unusable. A large part of the manpower and the machinery for various jobs – from silt clearance to solid waste collection – remain grossly under-utilised, while the low plant load factor of power generation plants has been a matter of serious concern for the policy-makers for many years. The only service that is more than fully, rather too fully, utilized is housing, which itself is a problem and which, probably, should not have been identified as a service in the first place. Civic authorities appear to be more interested in creating facilities and services than in their upkeep and optimum utilization. There have been cases where an enormous infrastructure – of water mains and underground sewers –

built at a massive cost, remained grossly under-utilised for several years, which in turn led to considerable erosion of their capacity, because owners of the adjoining houses could not afford the cost of connection to the mains; it took a long time for the civic authorities to wake up to the fact that it would make more economic sense to subsidize the cost of private connections immediately than to allow the entire investment to be virtually written off because of under-utilisation.

Third, generally speaking, when discussing urban problems issues relating to administration and maintenance tend to be ignored. There is a tendency to seek funds from various sources for development – which are more readily available – without taking into account their implications for regular maintenance expenses which are not usually provided for by the lending agencies. As a consequence, while civic infrastructure created with a lot of fanfare and publicity deteriorate quite rapidly, the civic authorities give more of their time and effort to seeking more development funds for new projects.

Fourth, the available services, net of leakages, are not spread uniformly over the citizenry. Their dispersion tends to favour the better off while slum dwellers, at the bottom of the social hierarchy, get only a fraction of what those in the top decile obtain. Compare the per capita water use in a luxury multi-storeyed building with that in a slum. Consider the fact that the amount of water used every time a toilet is flushed in a multi-storeyed apartment exceeds what is normally available to a slum-dweller in a day. Compare the bus-ride of an average citizen with the trip in a privately owned vehicle by the rich. Compare even the ability of the latter to bribe civic employees in order to keep their part of the road clean. Telephone connections in their flats are more quickly restored after any disruption, while they need no more than one phone call to get their gas cylinder replaced. The highly skewed distribution of various services is conspicuous practically in every city and town, and begs the question: urban development for whom?

Fifth, though the distribution of services is skewed, the charges and payments for various services are very seldom, if at all, linked to the quantum and quality of services obtained (except for private services or when informal payments are made for privileged access to regular civic services). Water rates are rarely imposed; even when these are in operation, the tendency is to link the water rate to the total rate as a proportion of the latter and not to actual water utilization. Water collected by way of high capacity private tubewells from underground sources is not usually subjected to such charges, despite the fact that it draws water from a common reservoir which is shared by local handpumps and shallow tubewells, and, some times, at the cost of supply to the latter which run dry. Similarly, the owner of private transport does not pay for the social cost of air pollution from the smoking exhaust, nor do the owners of the flats in high-rise buildings pay the full social cost of parking vehicles on the road. As a rule, the richer pay less for more of such services.

Sixth, a point which is closely linked to the main theme of this seminar, such development of infrastructure is seldom undertaken after consultation with the intended beneficiaries in various forms. In the early days of urban development, when the idea of slum clearance was advocated, it was assumed that the slum-dwellers would be pleased with a better accommodation at a distant place. It took urban planners quite some time to realise that (a) people in the third world prefer living in a community where every one is known to every one; and (b) they are averse to moving to new areas which are away from their place of work, particularly those engaged in informal sector self-employment. Women in a *bustee* would tell you where one drain does not match with another leading to waterlogging, where a tubewell or a street lamp should have been located to serve the maximum number, or whether a toilet or a public bath is a matter of higher social priority in an area. When old markets are redesigned and modernized, no effort is made to seek the opinion of those immediately affected – the sellers in the market and the buyers – either on the building plan itself or on the phasing of the programme which affects the functioning of the market, at the time of construction.

Having examined the problems, now let us examine the possible solutions.

How easy is it to expand the volume of such services? Let us admit, at the very outset, that many of the options have already been closed by the history of urban development. Generally, concern for urban planning comes very late in the life of a city. A city passes through many phases before it becomes a city, when its contours are shaped, its landscape gets formed and its settlements get firmly established. But it is not until a city becomes properly defined as a city and/or succeeds in gaining recognition as a municipality that the urban planner comes into the picture. By then the damage has already been done – no space has been left for parks, hospitals, clubs and other common facilities, roads have become narrow and their course zig-zagging, and houses have been built with virtually no consideration for aesthetics. Take the case of Calcutta. True that roads occupy only about six per cent of the total space, and there should be at least three times more space reserved for roads. But where is that space? To demolish houses in order to build wider roads and lanes is not a viable proposition: partly, because it would uproot many, and mostly poor who are on the brink of survival, and cause major social unrest, and, partly, because there is every likelihood of such a programme getting stalled for many years by way of a high court injunction. Take the problem of transport in this situation when adding more buses might actually lead to more time being spent in buses as the roads are already narrow and congested. These are problems that cannot be solved normally by way of urban planning. Nor would one welcome a great fire, which facilitated urban planning in London, or a war which having razed practically whole cities to the ground, made such planning possible in many of these in Europe or Japan.

Urban planning can still play an important role in the peripheries where space is more readily available. Nor should one fail to take note of the role played by the narrow, congested lanes of the city-core in some of the most modern cities in Europe today, where the tourists flock to see the historic buildings. In those city-cores, the lack of width is more than compensated by the cleanliness and shopping options that exist, and by the dynamism of the life around it. Once a city is viewed almost as a living organism with many different parts, each of these can be identified as playing a distinct and vital role and each adding colour to the collective urban life in its own ways. An overflowing city-centre is as much an integral part of the modern city landscape, as the wide roads and green avenues in the rest of the city.

Second, we should recognise that there are limits to what can be done to improve the civic services in isolation from the conditions of life in the hinterland. If the country is poor, and its rural population survives at the margin of starvation, this prescribes a limit on what can or cannot be done in terms of urban planning. This struck me vividly when, for a time, I was given the responsibility of drawing up a perspective plan for Calcutta. The senior engineers and architects of Calcutta Metropolitan Development Authority (CMDA) had by then drawn up a tentative plan for this great city. Assuming an additional 50 lakh population by the turn of the century, they worked out precise needs of housing, health, schooling as well as jobs that would be required at the perimeters of the great metropolis. We then asked a simple question: supposing we go through all these, build all the factories, schools, hospitals, houses, townships and parks to cater to the needs of the additional population, can we guarantee that we can hold the line at 50 lakhs? Can we be sure that five crores would not come, not only from the villages and towns of Bengal, but also from Bihar, Orissa, Uttar Pradesh, Assam, and, perhaps also, Nepal and Bangladesh? Once the word goes round that all the needs of those who manage to arrive in Calcutta would be taken care of, why should not the entire rural population of the Eastern Region crowd the pavements of Calcutta? Do we have the mechanism to stop it? This is simply not on. Calcutta would continue to look poor and not very pretty as long as the region as a whole remains poor. Any civic action that further widens the disparity between Calcutta and its hinterland would be negated by a fresh inflow of rural and small town population. The issue of balance, between the town and the periphery, can be overlooked only by making a mockery of the whole exercise of urban planning. Calcutta can only look pretty along with the rest of the region due to its umbilical links with of rural reality.

A third point to note is that, more often than not, a fund available for improving urban services would make urban services better and more accessible if, instead of spending it in urban areas, it is devoted to the development of rural areas. Many urban schools, colleges and hospitals carry a sizeable rural population, as also many factories and workplaces. In many cases, though not always, it would be cheaper to build and run a hospital or a good school in a rural area than to cater to their needs in the town, which would also involve travelling time and cost. In case of West Bengal, over the past 14 years or so, the development of decentralized Panchayati system, and its success in taking relief to the victims of flood or drought, wherever they are located, has significantly reduced the flow of disaster-induced migration to Calcutta and other major cities. It shows that, rather spending money on them as slum dwellers or as inhabitants of illegal squatting colonies, after they arrive in the town as destitutes or very poor, it is cheaper to spend on rural development and undertake activities which would make it possible for them to stay in the village. Unfortunately, given the way the government departments are organized, such inter-relationships are seldom taken into account when formulating policies; it would be hard to make the urban-based departments divert a part of their funding to rural development, even when, ultimately, such development rescues the towns and cities from overflowing rural migrants.

Fourth, nor should the ecological issues be ignored. In Calcutta, more or less exclusive concern with housing has led to the setting up of the Salt Lake City, while pressing transport needs have forced the construction of a metropolitan bypass along the eastern fringe. Taken together, these two prestigious and valuable projects have solved some major problems, but, at the same time, have created some new ones which were not clearly foreseen. For instance, the physical obstruction to the flow of water along the west-east slope in the city, caused by these projects, has intensified the problem of drainage in the low lying areas adjoining the bypass and the Salt Lake City. Further, the very construction of these two projects has led to the shrinkage of the salty water marsh area and is now acting as a powerful impetus for the further construction of houses in the area at the cost of the water bodies and greenery. For a city which is already heavily congested, and where green patches are rare to find, this further loss of open space and water bodies at the margin might have serious health and other implications. This rapid urbanisation has created another major problem in the same area of the city, where the dumping ground of solid wastes is also located, that is : where to find additional space needed for the expansion of the dumping ground which can cope with the increasing accumulation of waste. Shifting the dumping ground to a new place would create another environmental problem – that is in terms of heavy consumption of a non-renewable scarce resource, oil. Similar dilemmas are posed with respect to the question of establishing new settlements in the face of growing demand for housing in Calcutta. To settle them in East Calcutta is environmentally unacceptable, for the reasons given above, but to make them settle in distant towns along the north-south corridor would involve enormous additional energy costs in terms of commuting by train or bus, which too is ecologically unsound. A third alternative is to create urban settlements with independent economic base so that the additional energy costs in terms of commuting are dispensed with; but this is easier said than done as the case of Kalyani city illustrates.

Fifth, no matter what alternative is pursued, the nagging question of where to get funding from would remain. Issues connected with services are mainly State subjects under the Indian Constitution, yet the constitutional arrangement, regarding Centre-State distribution of fiscal power and financial resources, does not leave the State governments with sufficient funds to do justice to this constitutional obligation. The continuing dependence of all the States on the central government on practically anything important - from rural development,through literacy, to industrial development - reveals that there is something basically wrong with the distribution of financial and fiscal rights and powers between the States and the centre, which needs to be corrected. The National Commission on Urbanisation, in its interim recommendation, did make a note of this with reference to the four major cities in the country, when it said that the finance for their development should come mainly from the national government as the State governments would not have the financial strength to carry out those. While this recommendation – which, interestingly, was omitted from the final recommendation – was specific to a particular category of cities, the general point is valid, since, in the majority of cases, the budgets of the State governments would not permit large scale investments that are needed for developing urban infrastructure and services.

Having identified the major problems with regard to urban services and also the major constraints which stand in the way of their solutions, let us now examine the third element – the issue of popular participation.

I will begin by examining two types of *bustees* in Calcutta. The first are the usual *bustees* and *jhopris* where the squatters live. One notices a very high level of diversity in their social composition – in terms of language, religion, caste, village or area of origin, as also occupation. One also notices a high degree of skewness in their earnings – some, though living in the *bustees* for their own specific reasons, are quite well off, while the majority are day labourers, informal sector self-employed, etc., with income levels that barely keep them going. In this kind of *bustee*, developing community consciousness and making residents realize that they have some common goals – even keeping the waste in one place – is extremely difficult, though I know of quite a few in Calcutta where this very difficult task has been accomplished. The other type of *bustee* – most of which are no longer *bustees*, but were *bustees* in the late forties, fifties and even up to the seventies – are the colonies of the refugees from East Bengal, where people from a particular area congregated and where, therefore, social composition was homogeneous to start with. In the second type, even when they came as destitutes and lived in thatched houses with mud floors, one notices a certain amount of planning of space – a club room here, a *mandir* there, a school in the heart of the colony, with a park nearby, and a more regular ordering of roads with uniform space between houses. In the early days of their life in the city they revealed a very high degree of collective consciousness, in fighting the police and the authorities who were trying to evict them, in demanding rights to the land they had occupied and to various civic services, and also in imposing community-based self-discipline in the distribution of space to new squatters, taking into account their needs, etc. Such level of collective consciousness is not so evident in the refugee colonies now, since their rights have been recognized, they are no longer destitutes – the thatched houses with mud floor have become *pucca* ones – and the income distribution has become skewed.

This example also pin-points the problems that arise in securing popular participation. Compared to villages, the social and economic composition of the town population is highly diversified; the larger the urban area the greater is the degree of diversification. Take, for instance, Calcutta. In this great city, the rich own their own posh flat or house, ride their own private means of transport, send their children to more exclusive English-medium schools, and spend their spare time in elite social clubs where entry is restricted. The middle class mostly rent their accommodation or own a dilapidated structure, use buses or trams as their means of transport, and occasionally use taxi or rickshaw, send their children to ordinary schools and colleges, and enjoy their spare time in *para* clubs, libraries, *pujas* or in office-based organizations. The poor share the public transport with the middle class or walk, do not send their children to school or share the ordinary schools and colleges with the middle class, live in the *bustees*, and enjoy their spare time in their own set of clubs, cultural and religious activities. When these three categories interact, the relationship is usually formal and impersonal, and is based on master-servant or boss-subordinate kind of interaction. Leaving aside economic stratification, the urban population also tends to be segregated in social terms – religion, language and region – each having its own system of schooling, place of worship and social club. More often than not, such social segregation is accompanied by residential segregation. In the smaller towns, where a significant proportion of the population maintain close ties with their native villages – where they continue to own land or have family members, and from where relatives come to the town and go back – such village-based affinity often overrides loyalty to the urban areas where a person lives. All these illustrate how difficult it is to develop collective consciousness in the urban context, based on a town or city, or even a *para*.

Given the economically, socially and residentially fragmented nature of the urban population, what then could be done to ensure popular participation in developmental activities? Certainly, NGOs do have a role to play, but, in my opinion, the overall experience with the NGOs uptil now has been far from satisfactory, barring some with an excellent record and some community-based organizations. Even the best ones amongst these rely too heavily on charismatic leadership and wither away in the absence of such leadership. Further, these NGOs tend to rely too heavily on donors – whether missionary organizations or international development bodies or even the government departments – who decide on which programme to choose and how the activities are to be conducted, thus making them function as appendages of fund-giving bodies and taking away their 'voluntary' character. It has been also my experience, and I am sorry to say this, that the majority of the workers in most NGOs are not fired by any zeal for serving the people; they are there because alternative employment opportunities are scarce and leave as soon as something better comes their way. The NGO movement has not taken off in our country; let us accept this.

Another alternative is to rely on associations and cooperatives of employees. The latter play a vital role in the construction of housing, keeping the promoters at bay, while not making any demand on the State budget. LIG or MIG housing complexes also tend to do better in the upkeep of roads, planting of trees, running of the libraries and clubs, etc. Similarly, community-based organizations also tend to perform better, for the same reason. However, a major weakness with these organizations is that they are inclined to become parochial in their approach, and remain concerned with their own share of the urban space, some times at the cost of overall development of the town as a whole. I know of a case where an important extension of the bypass in Calcutta is facing stiff resistance from a local club and the neighbourhood because it would take away a part of the land that the former enjoys informally. There is a tendency to go to the court and seek injunction – which, surprisingly, they almost always get in their favour – and thus stall important urban projects, cause wastage of valuable time, which, in turn cause escalation of project costs, only because they would not permit relocation of some houses, shops or clubs.

Another kind of resistance comes up when people are asked to pay for the development they seek. The 'free rider' mentality is almost universal, as also the naive assumption that the government pays by cutting some one else's pocket and not mine. The property tax is a case in point. In most urban areas the value of a property tends to be under-assessed, for the purposes of property taxation, the main source of earning of the urban bodies; attempt by any civic body to raise realization from such tax by way of a more realistic assessment of property value is likely to face almost a rebellion, and the near certainty of the defeat of the party ruling in the civic body in the following election. I know of a canton in Switzerland whose offer of a reduction in rate was soundly defeated by the canton population in a referendum; the latter wanted the rate to remain but demanded better services. In India, we have a long way to go before we reach that stage of consciousness at the popular level. This is a case where we need political consensus, so the party in opposition does not make political capital of a valid increase in rates. The message should be brought home that urban development has a cost and those benefiting from it should pay, at least in accordance with the gains they make and what they can afford.

At the same time, let us admit, that a major reason for the lack of popular consciousness, for the people's inability to perceive urban issues in a broader context, lies in the way civic decisions are taken and the municipalities and corporations are governed. Those running the town hall tend to view the population as an object, and not as participants in the development process or as those who too have a role in decision-making. People are not involved, except at the time of voting, when they are fed with wrong information, and their most parochial and selfish instincts are pampered. People are never told in detail what the implications of a particular project are, what that would entail for their own life and what cost they themselves would have to bear to make it a success. Such projects are not seen by people as their own. But one can also find many examples where, once a project has been identified by the local population as their own, they have done everything to help its implementation and also its day-to-day operation.

People in Calcutta do not smoke in buses and cinema halls any more, because they know it is bad, and also because others would not allow it. Spitting in metro rail is rarely seen, because it is an object of pride, and anybody spitting would run the risk of being beaten up. During festivals millions participate for several days with the minimum disturbance. One wonders why the same self-discipline is not in evidence in preventing stealing of power from the highway main, stopping noisy music being played very late at night, making buses halt at every stop and only at scheduled stops, near the kerb and not in the middle of the road, discouraging throwing of garbage from the balcony, turning off the water tap after use, forming a queue whenever more than one person is seeking a particular service, or even in dissuading employees from giving bribes for getting what is due to them as a matter of course.

There can be no question that power should not be concentrated in running the civic administration. As far as possible it should devolve to smaller entities – from metropolitan bodies to towns, and within the towns from the town hall to the boroughs and other bodies closer to the citizens. More of the funds, fiscal power and rights should be transferred to them, so that they become responsible for their own good and more people get involved in the development process at the grass root level. This close association and local level consciousness, would always contain within it the seed of "localism", which a conscious and able leadership would have to overcome. It is possible that a closer involvement of the people with local level administration might give them a clearer idea of the financial, administrative and ecological constraints, and, thus, might make them more receptive to broader ideas and issues.

Let me also make it clear that the administrative solution suggested by the National Commission on Urbanisation would not work and would run counter to this spirit of popular participation. Their solution is to reduce the elected body to a purely deliberative assembly, while the real, decision-making power would be vested in a bureaucrat. The main argument behind such an obnoxious proposal is that the elected bodies tend to be quarrelsome, inefficient, partisan and corrupt, as if the bureaucracy in our country is highly efficient, free from corruption and does not get involved in squabbles or party politics. I would take the view that such problems can only be handled by way of regular elections coupled with popular participation in various forms, as also a very high level of public accountability, by providing the citizenry with the right to information, thus giving the latter the option, from time to time, to weed out the inefficient, corrupt and partisan. The proposed solution of the National Commission on Urbanisation is an autocratic one, which has never worked anywhere beyond a very limited time frame, while a solution which envisages popular participation at all levels of decision-making, by way of dissemination of all types of information, would have a much better chance of succeeding.

Lastly, let me make a point, as a student of economics, that the quantum and quality of services in a particular urban area would, in the ultimate analysis, be guided by the strength of the local economy. The landscape of a city is mainly shaped by the patterns of housing and transport. While the latter is mainly looked after by the State or the civic body, the former is usually a function of the level of living of the local population. If the economy of a city prospers, this is reflected in the private construction works, in housing, in the growth of the market, in the variety of goods available in the shops, and in many other hundred ways. This also provides the city authorities with the fiscal base for strengthening the civic infrastructure. If, on the other hand, the economy of the city is on the decline, no matter how much the civic authorities invest on infrastructure, it would continue to wear a shabby look. While discussing urban development, in particular infrastructural development, there is a tendency to overlook this overriding economic reality. This seminar, I hope, would take account of the social implications of such economic growth or decline, in terms of popular participation.

3

People and Municipal Services

M. N. Buch

The Indian Constitution, in its Preamble, states that it is the people of India who have constituted the Indian Republic. Sovereignty, therefore, vests in the people and all the constituent organs of the State, the legislature, executive and judiciary, have the sole function of helping the people to exercise their sovereign rights. So far as the organisational structure of the State, consisting of the Centre, the States and the urban and rural local bodies is concerned, this is merely an administrative arrangement to provide governance in accordance with the will of the people. There is nothing sacrosanct about the structure, which can be changed as required. The fact still remains that the administrative arrangements have the sole purpose of serving the people and promoting their welfare. This is as true of municipal administration as of any other level of government. Pivotal to the scheme of things is the people themselves. The people have certain expectations from the municipality and the right to demand satisfaction.

The laws setting up local government authorities lay down certain mandatory duties and functions, in which hygiene, sanitation,

Key-note address delivered at the Western Region seminar on "Urban Basic Services and Local Participation" organised by the Institute of Social Sciences in Baroda, April 1993.

prevention of infectious diseases, adequate and quality water supply, drainage and communication are given the highest priority. These mandatory functions are as good a definition of urban basic services as we can conceive. Every citizen has a right of access to adequate and safe drinking water, preferably through a water source within his own house, but in its absence through a public source which is protected from contamination and can provide a reasonable quantity of water to the user. The citizen has a right to demand that sufficient conservancy and sanitation arrangements be made to ensure that there is no dirt, filth, accumulation of garbage or nuisance created by lack of hygiene. He has an entitlement to such health care as will at least prevent infectious diseases. He is also entitled to maternity and child care, arrangements for the disposal of the dead and access to education for his children. The mandatory duties of the municipality, therefore, are matched by the entitlements of the citizen.

Dual Nature of Cities

What is the ground reality? Throughout urban India there are segments where those people live who have stability of occupation and income and for whom services have been provided over the years. The older parts of the cities, though serviced, tend to be a little more run down, the colonies of the rich have a degree of infrastructure, and new colonies, which have been planned, are constructed with a certain minimum amount of infrastructure, although completely lacking aesthetics. Together, these constitute the planned, serviced proportion of the town. Co-existing with it, economically integrated but totally segregated in infrastructural and social terms, is the vast, unplanned, non-city of the poor. Delhi and Indore, through the proliferation of unplanned, unauthorised settlements of the middle class, have achieved the miracle of a third element of city development, the non-city of the affluent. This duality between the planned city and the unplanned non-city is universal throughout urban India and a blot on our republic's escutcheon.

The unserviced portion of the city consists of slums, wholly denigrated and excessively densified portions of the old city where the services have collapsed, and the squatter colonies of the very poor and relatively recent migrants. These are the areas where even basic services do not exist or have only a rudimentary existence. These are also the areas where the municipality is not performing its mandatory functions and providing those services which the law demands compulsorily of it. These are, therefore, the areas where citizens are being denied their minimum entitlements and are being discriminated against.

The Seventh Five Year Plan document, has taken note of the mess in urban India. It states:

> The urban conglomerations, by their very nature, need a minimum of basic services for their healthy existence. However, the state of most of urban areas in this respect is far from satisfactory; in fact, in general the picture is extremely bad. Many of the municipal bodies have undeveloped and/or eroded tax systems and suffer from lack of capital funds for development. The services, if provided, have deteriorated over the years and there seems no sign of reversal. Over-crowded and under-serviced, an increasing proportion and area of urban conglomerations are being turned into slums. (*Seventh Five Year Plan*, [hereafter cited as SFYP] *Volume II*, Chapter 2, para 12.27).

Every urban settlement is under pressure on three counts. With a population growth rate which is more than double that of rural India and a sizeable annual in-migration, our large cities have become almost totally open-ended. The existing services are required to cater to more people every year, many of whom live on the periphery and at the end of, or beyond, the tail reach of the services. The second type of pressure is the ever increasing cost of maintenance, which has resulted in many of the services being run down for want of requisite repair and replacement. The third kind constraint, which is being felt even by the smaller towns with a fairly stable population, is that resources are drying up, both in financial and physical terms. A city such as Bangalore, for example, does not have a water source within easy reach which it can tap. When a service meant for X number of people is required successively to cater to X plus A on to

X plus Z, obviously the share of each citizen would be that much reduced. When core areas are redensified because of more intensive use of extremely valuable land, they draw off more than their fair share of such existing services as water and sewerage. At the same time the peripheral areas at the tail end of the services go on expanding, necessitating further extension of the existing services network, but without expansion of the head works and what flows therefrom.

Because of these pressures every municipality finds itself increasingly unable to provide even basic services to a large section of its citizens. Making a virtue out of necessity, several municipalities have almost abdicated their functions, pleading lack of rescurces for failure to look after the citizens. This despite the landmark judgment of the Supreme Court in the case of the Ratlam Municipality, in which the order of the sub-divisional magistrate under section 133 Cr. P. C. directing the municipality to remove a nuisance caused by lack of drainage was upheld by the court. The Supreme Court ruled that in the performance of its mandatory duties a municipality cannot plead lack of resources.

The Planning Commission has estimated that there are several States in which the coverage of the urban population by some form of protected water supply is less than 50 per cent. According to the Seventh Five Year Plan document:

> Although the average coveiage in the country is above 81 per cent, it is below 50 per cent in certain States. The above figures also do not reflect properly either the inadequacy of the water supply or the deprivation of the urban poor. The high rate of incidence of death and disease in urban poor settlements can be attributed largely to the poor quality of water and sanitation facilities (*SFYP, Vol. II*, Chapter 2, para 12.61).

Only about a third of the urban population is covered by any form of sanitation. Despite this, during the Seventh Plan only 01.60 per cent of the plan allocation was allotted to urban water supply and sanitation, all of it from the State sector, which is notorious for shortfall. The sheer helplessness of the Planning Commission in this regard is evident in the following words:

> Although the constraint of resources still continues, it is felt that the needs of the ... towns with regard to water supply and sanitation facilities can no longer be ignored. Therefore, augmentation and improvement of water supply facilities in the urban areas, especially in medium and smaller towns, will also have to be attempted during the Seventh Plan to the extent possible (*Ibid.*, para 12.60).

Considering the allocation actually made, the extent possible has been minimal indeed.

The National Commission on Urbanisation (NCU) in its report has brought into sharp focus not only the lack of basic services but also the inequality in distribution which further exacerbates the situation:

> Statistics regarding coverage of the urban population by public water supply and systems of hygienic conservancy do not give the whole picture. The States of Haryana, Tamil Nadu, West Bengal, Uttar Pradesh, Karnataka, Rajasthan, Gujarat and Madhya Pradesh have a general below average supply of water to urban centres. In much of Tamil Nadu and in large parts of Andhra Pradesh, especially in large cities such as Madras and Hyderabad, the water sources are totally inadequate to meet the demands of even the domestic sector, with the result that there is very limited piped supply and substantial recourse to alternative sources on an individual or community basis. Even in the capital city of Delhi there have been major water constraints and in many of the suburbs the water is either inadequate or of very poor quality. In most of the older urban centres the supply systems are well past their normal age-span and require major overhaul. In the document presented to the Commission by the Government of West Bengal it has been clearly stated that almost the entire distribution system of Calcutta requires replacement. Distribution is so inadequate and inequitable that,

while on the one hand those who have storage facilities are able to corner a major chunk of the water supply, a large proportion of the city population has to make do with public hydrants, intermittent piped supply of even drawal from non-municipal sources. More than the lack of water it is inadequate distribution which causes real problems. (Report of the *National Commission on Urbanisation 1988* [hereafter cited as *Report NCU*], Volume II, Part V, para 14.13).

The NCU has estimated that in order to provide water at 145 litres per capita per day in class I cities and 100 litres per capita per day in the rest of urban India, by the year 2001, approximately 16,000 million cu.m of water would be needed. As against the present supply of approximately 9500 million cu.m. we would need an additional 6,500 million cu.m. of treated, piped water supply. By the year 2001 we would have to invest approximately two lakh crores of rupees in water supply alone. The total outlay for water supply and sanitation in the Seventh Plan was Rs. 2935.64 crores, which is less than four per cent of the required outlay. Such a huge investment is clearly beyond us.

It is for this reason that the Commission has recommended new supply norms of between 70 and 90 litres per capita per day for domestic purpose, with another 30 to 40 litres per capita per day for non-domestic use. Great emphasis has been placed by the Commission not so much on the increase in water supply as in improving the distribution system so that existing supply could reach the poorest households in the city.

Strengthening Local Government

The present trend of thinking is that government cannot possibly perform the task of providing services and, therefore, these should be transferred to private enterprise or left to non-governmental groups, which should provide the service with people's participation. I would like to dissent from the opinion that municipalities need not be made to efficiently provide municipal services and that they should be relieved of this function. I am a votary of efficient administration.

It is the function of any government to govern and local government is no exception to this. What ails our municipalities? Because municipal government has been downgraded in stature through supercession, hamstrung in the matter of the resource base and supplanted by functional agencies such as developmental authorities, water supply undertakings, etc. local government has lost its elan. Even the City Corporation of Bombay no longer attracts politicians of the stature of Dadabhai Naoroji or Pherozeshah Mehta. The poor quality of the elected representatives has resulted in most municipalities being unable to think beyond their respective noses. In any case, local government is now left so bereft of revenue sources that long term city planning becomes an exercise in futility. Two examples will suffice to illustrate the point. Karnataka and Madhya Pradesh abolished octroi and replaced it by a grant-in-aid guaranteed by the State government. In the case of Bangalore, grant-in-aid accounts for about 80 per cent of the municipal corporation's revenue and in Madhya Pradesh the average figure is about 60 per cent. The remaining tax base is so narrow that there is no incentive to enhance it. In Karnataka over the past few years the first victim of the straitened resources of government has been the grant in lieu of octroi, and in Madhya Pradesh in the last financial year government was unable to release the full grant to the local bodies. Under these circumstances it is not surprising that local government is moribund and unable to fulfil its mandatory duties.

The NCU has commented at length on the need to strengthen local government and make it truly participative:

> Our system of democratic government bestows on the 'people' the ultimate power and our socialistic society professes the goal of equal opportunities and freedom of expression to all, making 'people' the subject and also the instruments of development. There are other compelling reasons, in the context of present-day Indian city reality, which makes people's participation an important component of city governance and development action. Our cities are in deepening crisis, finding expression in: (a) their failure to grasp the nature and dimensions of the economic crisis that grips them and to respond to its challenge in

a planned, positive manner; (b) their loss of conflict-resolving instruments which lay traditionally in their social institutions and arrangements; (c) the collapse of urban leadership, both among the people and in formal institutions of city administration and development planning which has lowered the quality of decision-making and forward planning, resulting in loss of direction and deterioration in quality of living, nature of development and delivery of services; and (d) the cities' failure to respond to the challenge of urban poverty. It is this crisis that gives the theme of people's/ community/public/citizen participation an entirely new dimension. People's participation, in the context of present-day urban reality, is no longer a 'liberal ideal', it is a compelling necessity. (*Report NCU, Vol. II*, Part VI, para 16.1.1).

Rationalised Structure of Local Government

People's participation has to begin with an active interest by all citizens in municipal affairs. It is in this context that the NCU had recommended that large cities, with a population of more than half a million each, should have a two-tier system, in which local functions are assigned to a directly elected local council and city-wise functions vest in an indirectly elected corporation. The jurisdiction of the local council should be compact enough for the average citizen to be able to interact with the authorities. The local council should have some independent powers of taxation and surcharge on corporation taxes, while receiving an equitable share of city revenues, thus enabling a more enterprising council to enhance the quality of life of citizens, with their willing support for additional resource raising.

The point calls for elaboration. The NCU was of the view that, by and large, towns with a population of less than half-a-million tend to be single cored and are amenable to management as a single unit of administration. Cities larger than this tend to be polynodal, multi-cored, highly complex in their activities and amenable to division into semi-independent townships or colonies. In such cities direct interaction between citizens and the administration becomes difficult. Hence it is possible to categorise functions as those which are indivisible and those which can be decentralised at local levels.

The indivisible functions would be overall financial planning and management, city planning in the context of the city region and such services as the transport system, mains water supply and sewerage, power, etc. Citywide land management, environmental protection and pollution control are also centralised functions. Local roads, parks, schools, street lighting, scavenging, recreational facilities, environmental hygiene, etc., are all functions which can be decentralised at local levels and, because they directly affect the average citizen, be placed under the control of a local organisation with which the average citizen can interact. It is in this context that a two-tier level of municipal administration was suggested by the Commission, whereby the corporation, not being involved in routine municipal administration, could do a professional job of planning, raising resources and providing citywide basic services. The local council, on the other hand, could perform all the routine municipal functions and be held directly accountable to the people. The people then could insist that the municipality functions efficiently, uses resources wisely and responds positively to the needs of the people.

If the local councils and corporations are organised in such a way that the councillors meet after normal working hours, it should be possible for professionals, service personnel, etc., to participate in municipal government. There should be no restriction on a government servant standing for local government election, with the police and senior officers of the district administration being excluded. It is only when the quality of the councillors improves that one can expect efficiency in local government.

Community Management and Responsibility

In Japan there is a system of community management of local services, such as street sweeping, garbage collection, maintenance of environmentally sensitive areas and gardens, etc. Tasks are assigned to every family living in a locality and one finds the footpath being hosed down by one group of housewives, roadside planters being attended by another group and garbage being neatly packaged and stacked by yet another. In India we have yet to develop such a sense of community participation. We need a very strong community development programme in every city in India, managed by the citizens themselves and not bureaucratised as has happened in some cities.

Throughout Europe one finds that local government leases out tiny plots of wasteland within the city and on its periphery for the development of gardens, which are tended over the weekend by the citizens. Berlin is a very good example of this. A person living in a block of flats thus obtains a tiny piece of land, a few hundred square feet in area, where he rids himself of tension by reverting to nature. These weekend gardens substantially improve the city environment because of the vegetables, flowers and fruits grown thereon. Every Indian city has plenty of wasteland, at present an open invitation to encroachment and public defecation. It might be worth considering leasing out of small patches, say 200 sq. metres each, to people who would use them for gardening. This could also be done by making the land available to the locality, whose community organisation could then determine how it will be used in an environment friendly manner. Provided we are able to prevent illegal construction on such land, we could greatly improve the city environment without any cost to government.

I have had the good fortune of managing the affairs of three cities, Ujjain, Bhopal and Delhi, where I learnt certain important lessons. One of them is that nothing should be given free, even to the community. Almost 30 years ago when I was both Collector of Ujjain District and Administrator of the City Corporation, I decided that public stand posts would not be made available without community participation. This meant that first the community had to organise itself, then the cost of the service would be worked out, followed by an assessment of affordability. If the cost was X and affordability X - Y, then the latter amount had to be deposited with the corporation. Thereafter a nominal monthly charge had also to be paid by the users of the service. The community was collectively responsible for maintaining the stand posts, including replacement of any missing parts. Despite initial resistance by the politicians the system took off and we found that the community jealously guarded the facility which had thus been made available, largely because it felt that the service having been paid for was now a right they were entitled to. Similarly, in Delhi I refused to regularise unauthorised colonies unless they paid development charges. Taking the example of one such a colony, Santnagar, the community refused to pay the charge because, as the leaders put it, they did not trust us to utilise the funds properly. On my meeting the deadline regarding water supply as per an agreement between us, the residents of Santnagar paid the balance of the development charges within 24 hours. In other words, a community will cooperate with local government only if it is convinced that the declared goods will be delivered. If it is the responsibility of the authorities to ensure this, it is equally the responsibility of the community to insist upon this.

There are certain areas in which local participation may be the best method of delivery of basic services. These would be distribution of water, sanitation, the maintenance of such common properties, as playgrounds and gardens, preventive health care and pre-primary education. Here the municipal authorities must first create a basic community level organisation of the people living in a locality which can take on the responsibility of looking after these services. So far as maintenance is concerned, the municipal share of the cost should be transferred to the community which would then be responsible for their upkeep. We need not get unduly upset by misapplication of funds in a few localities. If the community leaders misapply the funds let them account for their failure to the community rather than to city government. No one can become too rich on the small amounts involved, but community leaders would place themselves at personal risk if the local level services were not maintained. To illustrate this by an example, in 1965, Madhya Pradesh faced an unprecedented drought. While reducing the mains water supply to the city of Ujjain, I repaired more than 50 wells and installed pump sets on them that were connected to overhead tanks with community taps. The key of the motor was handed over to the local community leader, who was responsible for filling up the overhead tank as per the capacity of the well. Because water was thus available on tap locally, even if in limited quantities, there was no panic and we were able to pass through the summer quite comfortably. This is a good example of municipal-people cooperation.

Private Enterprise Contribution

Does private enterprise have a role to play in providing city services? All business tends to take advantage of the economies of scale and concentration, described by Shri Sanat Mehta as the economies of urbanisation. If business were to contribute to municipal coffers in proportion to the economies of urbanisation enjoyed by it, the equilibrium would be maintained. In truth, however, business, especially manufacturing industry, locates itself in the city or its immediate vicinity, uses the existing services, contributes virtually nothing to municipal taxes by locating outside municipal limits, and brings the existing physical and social infrastructure of the city under unbearable strain. Business, thus, passes on its entire social overheads to the city. According to the NCU:

> There are two levels at which this happens. One is in the existing city or town, which already has some infrastructure available to service the population. Obviously, there are certain economies of scale and concentration which prevail, very succinctly referred to by Sanat Mahta as the economies of urbanisation. This is a new term of which the Commission would like to take note. Business locates where there are economies and this makes good economic sense. If business were to contribute in equal measure, immediately and in the long run, to city coffers, the services would be maintained at a reasonable level of efficiency. However, what generally happens is that business, especially manufacturing industry, locates in the city or in its immediate vicinity and uses the existing services. If the business is located outside municipal limits there is no contribution by it to municipal taxes. At the same time the existing stock of housing is used by the workers; water supply, sewerage and drainage are brought under greater pressure; the transportation system is over-extended; the social infrastructure of education, medical care, etc., is stretched beyond endurance; and, in short, the entire social overheads of business are transferred to the city. The general picture throughout India is that such expansion, while it may create jobs, also imposes a burden on the city services, for which there is no commensurate payment.

> Economic activities in cities causes an increase in population, proliferation of slums, increased pressure on city services and their general running down. In a way this is the urban paradox in India. As the wealth of a city increases through new investment, the look of the city becomes more and more ugly and the level of municipal services continuously declines. The Commission feels that this is the result, partially, of the irresponsibility of business and partially of the weakness of government which fails to make business pay for the social infrastructure which it uses.
>
> The economies of urbanisation, which should really be treated as a social resource, are thus converted into a private resource by the businessman. The social wealth of the city has been created over generations, through taxes, State intervention and private donations. It is this social wealth which is privately appropriated because new business does not participate in its upkeep and upgradation. The Commission very strongly feels that this trend has to be reversed and business should be made to participate in the process of creating new social assets (*Report NCU, Vol. II*, Part III, Paras 7.4.2, 7.4.3 and 7.4.4).

Private enterprises must participate in city improvement and the maintenance of services. Once again I could not put it better than in the words of the National Commission on Urbanisation:

> The Commission is of the view that merely restricting the location of the business is not enough. In the ultimate analysis these restrictions are bypassed by any business which sees profit in locating in a large city. Instead, fiscal measures should be used to force the business to take into account the cost of the social infrastructure while estimating the profitability of the venture in a city location.
>
> Some suggestion in this behalf are:
>
> (i) Changes in the Central, State and municipal tax structure whereby new businesses locating in and around large cities or towns are made to contribute substantially to revenues.

(ii) A system of tax incentives whereby, to the extent that the business invests in housing, infrastructural development within a given locality and the construction and maintenances of such social infrastructure as schools, hospitals, etc., there are heavy tax rebates, if need be up to 100 per cent in suitable cases. Such rebates could also be extended it the business undertakes conservancy measures in a given locality.

(iii) If business grants assistance to its employees for construction of private or co-operative housing, suitable tax rebates could be considered.

(iv) If a business locates outside municipal limits, to be extent that its workers commute over municipal services, it must be taxed as if it is located within the municipality. If the municipality cannot legally apply the tax, then the State government should do so and pass on the revenues to the local body responsible for providing services. (*Report NCU, Vol. II, Part III*, Paras 7.4.6 and 7.4.7).

If new industrial towns are created because of locational policies or setting up of resource specific industries the Commission has suggested that when the land is allotted it should be so priced that the capital cost of township development is recovered therefrom. In the case of Pithampur in Madhya Pradesh it was found that 2000 hectares of land was alloted to industry at Rs. 1.5 lakhs per hectare The total investment in industry is Rs. 2,000 crores. If the land had been valued at Rs. 7.5 lakhs per hectare an additional Rs. 120 crores could have been raised, which would have more than met the cost of township development. This would have added a mere six per cent to the cost of industry. Similarly, if industry is assigned the pro rata cost of development, with such investment being tax deductible and the resources thereof being made available by the financial institutions which provide investment capital, we could ensure proper township development at the cost of private enterprise. In other words, it is not so much the transfer of municipal services to private hands which is called for, rather the devising of means whereby those who make private profit should contribute towards the provision of city services.

To sum up, a participative approach to providing basic services, first and foremost, calls for citizens demanding that the municipality will perform its mandatory functions. It also calls for a willingness on the part of citizens to contribute directly to municipal resources. Many of the services are amenable to decentralised management at community level and a system of community participation must be developed in each locality.

Thereafter, local government must be prepared to trust the community and to devolve maintenance funds to it. Such decentralised management of municipal services would improve efficiency and still retain the services in the public domain, instead of transferring them to organisations whose sole interest is profit.